Applaud
the
Chains

Jessica Marion King

Fulton Books
Meadville, PA

Published by Fulton Books 2023

ISBN 979-8-88731-571-3 (paperback)
ISBN 979-8-88731-572-0 (digital)

Printed in the United States of America

To my Uncle Jack and Aunt Jean,
Who never gave up on me and praised me.
RIP Uncle Jack
Love, Red

Uncle Jack

It seems like I only see you every so often
Like a wave to the sand goes by and softens
You're a hero, a father, a miracle to me
You're the only one that calls me red and sees me
I wish you would get better; I wish you were here
Silently patting my head and whispering how much you care
You're like a father to me, Uncle Jack, and
I don't take these words back
So join me now and say a prayer that will keep you safe forever
No more bad times, just you and me together

Fall

Red leaves in a tree
They are falling
Falling crimson, regret, and despair
The red on the leaves drips like wet paint
Until they cover the ground like wet blood
Moving in the wind so gently
Then it turns to a deadly spin
Moving faster and faster
Then all dies

Daddy

You were never there for me
You made me feel lost and forgotten
I cry in the depths of my soul
My heart carries a heavy load
But I'm your little girl, Daddy, can't you see
But you're blinded by your remorse and selfishness
Just the thought of you made my eyes sting
Was it something I did?
Did I do something wrong?
You tell me
Why couldn't you have been there for me, Daddy?
Why'd you have to leave?
Feels like you stabbed me over and over again
Me wishing you happiness
But in return me getting pounded by your words
Can't you see, Daddy, I love you
Can't you see I just want a family?
But you've taken that from me
Like everything else
Goodbye, Daddy
I can't love you anymore

Breakthrough

Sunshine breaking through the glass
I reach off and take off your mask
I see regret, terror, demolishing pieces
In your eyes are the signs of masterpieces
It is hard to explain where you are from
I know that your insides are numb
But the tremble of anguish is at your stance
I look at you back from a mirror and look at you half glance

Romance Despair

With this hand, I will tremble
With my feet, I will stumble
I have seen a great many deals of life
Experiences have shown me peace and strife
I look up to the clouds and see black smoke
One in which makes me choke
Fall back down and let me rise
This is my rhyme so I will summarize
That romance despair is me
And it won't let me be
I dance, I sing, I clap my hands
But it is all the same in distant lands
Where there is no time to be free but demolished
That is when I will remain and be honest

Repair

Repair me not for I am undone
Sing a song and make me young
Establishment is at my fingertips
But remorse is in my soul in tiny bits
How can I repair myself if I am not okay?
Wait for it, it will better in the month of May
Tired, stressed, and I don't have a clue of what to do
So I say the rest is up to you

Demolition

Shatter my soul and make me new
Then stick me back together like glue
Blood rushes through my veins seems all right
But I have a world to fight
It is a power that lengthens my dreams
Then puts me together like seams
Demolition is a curse in which you have to hurt
But it doesn't have to be unless you are alert

Winter

Winter news comes to an end
But I feel likely to stand again
With birds chirping and flowers blooming
I feel at rest in my new beginning
The snow will melt one day
But today is not that day
I say your name at a stop
But my voice is heavy like carrying a wet mop
Frozen things linger in the woods
But I will not go even if I could
Winter is sad in a time of sorrow
Maybe it'll be a better tomorrow

Grateful

I am surprised with all I have
Even if I feel bad
I linger in darkness even if the sun is shining
However, I am grateful to be alive and thriving
With a home, a mom, and a sister who cares
I am all but bare
With freedom that approaches me from above
I will succeed and show light like a dove

Watch me

Watch me, watch me
Watch me die
Watch me, watch me
Watch me cry
See me entering a room
See me in a gloom
Acid of tears below the ground
Acid of tears makes no sound
I am the legend of all cries
I am the girl that says goodbye

Stitches

There they go
Stapling below
My skin ripping apart
Breaking my heart
The knife that once was is now lost
The staples that were once there
Remain a scar that is bare
It'll be there forever
Until the pain is over

Blood

That irony taste in your mouth
So luscious to the touch
How beautiful the color
We see it more during summer
A waterfall of red
Coming from her neck
Is never pretty
So sit back and bleed

Yelled

She yelled at me and made me cry
I deserve to die
Swallowed by a black hole
She has crushed my soul into tiny pieces
And folded my brain into tiny creases
I must change my way of living
Otherwise she remains screaming

Disappointment

I never get anything right
You see me fail in plain sight
I'm worthless and ashamed
I am the one to blame
If people didn't doubt me
Maybe I'd do things right
But then again, my mistakes are there
They leave me empty and bare
So I cry on the inside
Hoping no one sees on the outside
With failure written all over my face
I feel unsafe
But I remain human
And that's all

Knife

Temptation is there
Holding the knife is all I saw
Until slowly…knife breaks skin
Blood slowly gushing out
You want to die
Falling to your knees
You draw your last breath
Then…

Beloved

Beloved stars
Beloved bars
Beloved chains
Beloved stains
Beloved hearts
Beloved parts
After all beloved is a new start

Hatred

The feeling of anguish in you
The feeling of starting something new
Hopefully this hatred will be over
Otherwise it stays with you forever
Climbing down rocks to get to your path
Seems as difficult as doing math
But you remain still
And hope the sun will rise but still until

Alive

I'm alive
I feel it inside
With me breathing deep breaths
And my heart pumping in my chest
I feel somewhat all right
Even though I am a little affright
Saying these words is possible
But being alive is impossible
How can I reach this climax?
If you only ask
Is this for real?
I fight my insides like a thousand men
And hope that I will mend

Feel

Blankness, emptiness, helplessness,
Shyness, cautious, jealous,
What I feel is who I am
What I say is where I stand
Hoping to feel relief
Hoping to have a belief
Shouting out my name
Never staying the same
Relief is coming upon me
Now I am free

My Jealousy

It's like when you heart is all crushed up inside
Harder and harder to breathe
Agony is taking over
All the happiness in the world comes to an end
You see your future in another way
Come, come for you will see
The pain in which you already know

Handle

Some things you just have to be patient with
Waiting for someone can cause your mood to switch
But in the depths of my soul, it's hard to maintain that urge
I want to bolt out and cry with such surge
My heart squeezing tightly in my hollow cage
It just wants to burst out in outrage
But here I'll wait and sit
And I'll admit
That it's hard to control my soul

Regret

I don't know how I could have done it
I do have a lot of pain that nobody has experienced
All my trust is taken away
Maybe they'll trust me some other day
My injury hurts so bad
I could not be more mad
This is my mistake that I have to face
Hopefully one day I'll fall into grace
It broke my family's heart once
But I did it anyways
I have nothing left to say

Dying

Like when your stomach melts
I feel my pencil, that was the last thing that I felt
Every bone in my body hurts
Blood is on my shirt
I feel my body moving away from life
I keep telling myself it is all right
At least I'll be happier
But right now couldn't hurt any worse
I need air away from my thoughts
My brain is completely clot
Someone help me please

Complicated

My life is so simple
Until you look at the big picture
I'm blamed for other's actions
You'll believe me once you see her reaction
My time and thoughts wonder away
Until I have something to say
I am led astray
Until I see the monthly bills she pays

Vanish

One day you'll see me
The next you won't
I have died
You remain shy
I have moved into a bliss
That you surely won't miss
My life is worthless
So I'll sing out and regard this

Snapped

I am nice, right?
I may bug people at extreme heights
But all I want to do is talk to someone
But all I get is shunned
Doesn't anyone see?
I'm lonely, I plea
So when you snap at me
I can't stand me

Mom

Mom may shout and scream
But when she smiles, it gleams
She's the most wonderful mother in the world
Even though she had a hard time when she was a girl
I can't help but thank her for everything she's done
She's in my heart and I'll never let her go
She may drive me crazy
But I love her so

Exploring

Exploring my mind
Makes me kind
I obsess over the human brain
Which fascinates my smears and stains
I conjure up ideas and emotions
Which make me have options
That I can share with the world
But I am one girl
That can do this task
But I only ask
Is to open up to me
And let it be

My Special Place

My special place is dark and sad
With an imagination that should be glad
Every thought is crowded and safe
Inside my mind is full of wonder and no escape
My mind is distinctive and atypical
I stay in my inclination and remain typical

Countless

Countless times I thought of suicide
Countless times I've thought of how to die
If you add it all up, I should be in a hospital by now
So everyone take a bow
And look back up
The countless of times I thought these things
Ran a muck
So pray for me please
Otherwise I will scream
Your name
Countless of times
It's all the same
So here I lie
By your bedside

Sideways

Up and down
Backward and forward
Then sideways
Because I have a disorder, I am sideways
I see things differently
A different perspective maybe
Does sideways make me crazy or sane?
If I fall, I will stab the earth
My sideways notion is a new birth
That has seen many things
Creations and endings
But now I will go backward
And see what I have entered

Obsession

I obsess over things
That aren't necessary
But to me they are everything
Like books and journals make me wonder
I want to explore my emotions and slumber
So let me fill the pages of my thoughts
And let me keep all that I bought

Bulletproof

You may judge me
You may laugh at me
But I will me stone
So when you point your words at me
Then FIRE!
I will stay in place and wonder
But I have discovered
That bulletproof is my name
You may hit me, scratch me, it is all the same
For I wear a shield that protects
I'm no longer a tiny insect
But a big boulder that has forces beyond control
Your words have gotten old

The Devil's Kiss

As God made me
The devil kissed me
That's why I have bipolar
And other problems that seem to go on as I grow older
He cursed me with this turmoil
It makes me tick and boil
The devil does this to all people
Even to Jesus in the little steeple
It makes me wonder how he gets away with it
This is my story and belief so keep it
But the devil has some gifts at your birth
Knowing that makes me hurt

Liar

She moves
She stares
She smiles
She's there
Telling stories all the time
To help her unwind
But what she says is a lie
She doesn't do it all the time
But mostly wants to excite
Keep people entertained
Because her life is actually boring and lonely
And not the same from you and me
She has secrets that she can't share
So she lies to their faces and pretends life is nonexistent
So are the lies really lies or cover-up?
You tell me!

A challenge

To wake everyday
Seems the same
To watch the birds fly away
It's like they never came
To watch my day in tears
Seems okay
Listening to my fears
Makes me outraged
A challenge every day to feel sane
To keep a secret that is your very being
To run and hide when things get bad
To sell yourself short all the time
To feel your moods and no one else cares
It's a challenge to lay in bed
Thoughts climb in your head and swirl around
They dance until you forget your name
What does it mean to be bipolar?
What does it take to make it over?
My challenge is everyday
And I never feel the same

Reputation

Who cares?
Who's there?
Everyone stares
One mistake and your life is done
One mistake and your life is gone
Reputation defines who you are
But if you screw it up
Your life is in misery
I mean it, seriously
Some people don't care about their reputation
But I consider it a connection
To the human world
Ruin this chance
Forget romance
And live with laughter in your ears
Insecurity is there
So sit in the corner
And be scared
Life is over as we know it
Life was perfect before reputation was made

Veins

Unlocking the secrets
That course through your veins
One little item that suppresses your brain
Blue blood pours through your system
Hear the blood flowing and listen
The calming ripple through your veins
The heat of blood keeps you sane
One little vein will go a mile
The taste of blood will make you smile
So look beneath your skin
And see what's within
Each vein contains a secret that explodes
When you puncture a vein, it erodes
Your body is special
Treasure it for its confidential

Hurt

That feeling in your stomach so deep within
When someone knows your secret
Your heart swims
Taking you for granted
Hurts the most
Knowing your secrets is like dancing with a tornado
It's risky, it's dangerous
It's out of control
You're on your own
With thoughts in your head
That don't settle down
Until these words are said
The hurt in your system
Won't cover that hole
Until you're comfortable
With your own soul

Better

Your life doesn't have to be depressing and sad
I know how you feel inside your mind
Take it from me, it would be better to smile more
But it's your choice
Don't single you out
Because the whole point is better to say
I've done it
It's a cruel lesson to deal with the obvious
But saying I beat bipolar
I beat anxiety
I beat my thoughts
I beat self-injury
Makes you feel better inside
Knowing you're alive

Weird inside

When I'm manic
I panic
I feel like my heart has two beats
It's like my bones are rattling nonstop
I'm happy and smiley
But I bug others simply
I am talkative to the end of the earth
Feels like I'm on waves so I surf
What helps me is nothing
This pattern won't go away
Being manic isn't fun anymore
Feels like I could jump five feet or more
I want to talk to someone so badly
But they ignore me sadly
My weirdness inside makes my breathing fast
Makes me want to go back into the past
And settle down at last

Ready to Die

Sitting and waiting
Waiting and sitting
To the end of life
To the start of life
I am ready to die
To face my fears of heaven and hell
To be one with myself and all around me
But you will see
The matters which hold me together
And sleep in a deep slumber
Am I worthy of all my being?
I have accepted the truth behind walls
That there was no life at all
So ready or not, I'm going to die
Even if I haven't finished the design
I am ready

Uncontrollable

Sometimes I get in these moods
Where I shout and scream
And bang my knees
My imagination conjures up a plan
To be sarcastic and mad
To others around
I make a lot of sound
But nothing can stop
The uncontrollable force within
My imagination is a scary place
Once I wish to leave and forget
And say goodbye to this list

Done

I'm done with this
I'm done with that
I'm tired of cleaning up this mess
What will it take for you to see?
That I'm human and want mercy please
You make and feel small and insignificant
Can you hear my chant?
I'm in dire need of self-courage
I'm done with everything you say about me
So let me flee
And get out of your way
This is what I have to say
That in the month of May
I'll be okay
To rest in my coffin
And hear my voice soften
But I'm done

Never calls

I wait by the phone to hear it ring
Like waiting for a silent scream
It'll never happen, you see
She's neglected me
I just want to hear her voice
But answering is her choice
I don't see her everyday
I wish I could but sadly she is away
It's like she's in the mist
And it doesn't recognize her
It's like I'm deaf without her
But still sadly I wait by the phone
And I will be alone
She's my best friend
My only friend
And still she never calls even if I plea
She doesn't get the message I see

Lost

I'm lost, can't you see?
I just want to grow up and gleam
But in the depths of despair the light goes out
There is no one to hear me shout
I'm lost in these cell walls
That cumulate my brain
There is no answer
Only questions
Still, I'm a lost child within
Feels like I must hold my breath to scream
When will this go away?
When will it be May?
Never

May

May is when the trees fall
May is when you have nothing at all
It's the time when roses die
It's the time when you can't see the sky
It's that time of month for that little girl's birthday
But she doesn't have much to say
May has the silent scream
It makes the girl impossible to dream
She has no family it seems
So May is a miserable month
That everyone wants to forget
Especially for that girl

Kiss

Kiss me, Kiss me
I want someone to kiss me
Waiting for a guy
Who will kiss me by surprise
Hoping the feeling feels good
Waiting for that moment
When I'm in the right mood
But when will this time happen?
Are my lips misshapen?
I realize that I'm not that pretty
You can say, more likely ugly
But I put myself out there
And see who cares

# *Waste My Time*

I won't waste my time on you
I won't waste my rhyme on you
This is the last poem I write about you
I swear this is true
Your ups and downs make me seasick
Your anger and frustrations bother me
It's like I'm on a roller-coaster ride
Except it goes on forever and ever
I waste my time trying to help you
But really all I'm doing is kidding myself
To a point where I hate myself
This is the last poem about YOU!

Emily

Your smile shines brighter than the sea
Your eyes glimmer more than the sky
I wish you could be around all the time
To hear your laugh makes every flower bloom
Why do you have to go so soon?
You and I have grown so fast
It seems like we barely had a past
Hopefully our memories will stay with you
You're a great person and have so much to give
Read this poem when you're down
You're an amazing person, Emily
Just keep going and you'll succeed
Just know that I'm proud of you

Don't Care

That feeling inside
Where you can't hide
Where that special place
Is now unsafe
Your jaw clenches hard
Like hearing a sharp shard
What happened to that moment
Where everything made sense
So confused you don't know what to do
Waiting for the light to shine
But all I do is whine
I want to care again
To feel the raindrops' revenge
To know what it is like to be free
To know what it is like to see

Before the End

I write a letter saying goodbye
I have tears that shed no lie
I look around me and the room is bare
It feels like the walls look and stare
How can I cope with this default?
This suicide will be all my fault
I sit on the floor and wait for help
This waiting is like greeting a belt
Finally, I sit and think of my actions
No better reason to die than my bleak reactions
So here's to death all in my skull
Here's one final shove and pull
I am dead on the floor
No more pain, I'm sure

Cannot Escape My Fate

Twisting and turning
My insides burning
My heart pounds
For it is bound
My emotions play
So say hurray
But still I cannot escape what's in me
The way of conviction
That possesses each thought
I'm locked away and can't find my place
This is my fate
That I can't escape
Holding my own hand, I pray for oblivion
To mourn the ground beneath
Then to see the sunrise that I beseech

Change

Walking on hot stones seems okay
Seeing the sun rise is just another day
But changing is the hardest part, you see
It makes things all blurry and funny
Being who you are is difficult and hard
It's like carrying a ton of lard
Tears well up in your eyes
Break this curse for this hurts
Being all alone
Trying to understand what people are telling you
Too much information to take
Maybe you were a mistake

Solid

Can't see through me
Can't see around me
Reading my face tells no lie
But seeing my insides you'd die
To know I'm an emotional wreck
Others see my crime and connect
The dotted lines don't appear to match
So I leave one scratch
To perform my new task
That relies on you
To discover what is true

Disappointment

I am a disappointment
It happens in certain moments
With the flesh I bleed and the terror I scream
There is something wrong with me
I cannot help who I am
But I can help with what I do
Outside I may seem like a sweet child
But inside the devil plays his part
I can only blame this on one person…
Me

Monster

Monsters in my head and brain ready to start
Come out to play and remind me your skin is like bark
No matter what I do
To get rid of you
Out of the question
This monster lives in me
I hear it roar and scream
It's my shadow
It's my face
It's my hair
It's what I taste
My monster lives beneath my skin
In my bones that sticks to me like paste
It conjures up emotions
When I let it go
All hell breaks loose
Otherwise I keep it caged
To stay sane
I let it loose in the month of May
So I can be like everyone else, the same

Come Out, Come Out
Wherever You Are

I know you're there
Seeking behind wisps of your hair
Standing up straight
Hiding your face
But deep within your soul is unsafe
Capturing the image that is black and blue
Feeling insecure, what do you do?
I say this because you're just like me
Wondering around aimlessly
Seeking a development
Holding your own hand to get comfort
So instead of hiding
Come out wherever you are!
Show me the scratches
Show me the time
Show me what you do to stay alive

Spending

Spending is not my greatest creation
My spending is an abomination
That hovers over me like a cloak
It's so addicting like having coke
My treatment doesn't define the need
But the need to feed my credit card is up to me
I realize the task at hand is trickier than the desire to stand
Stop for it doesn't help
Every purchase has the task to make me yelp
I need certain things
More a want actually
But I see through my eyes something I cannot control
It will not define who I am but what I am not

Help

Help! For the is tragic
Help! For this is strategic
Help! May I find peace that lives in exile
How can I overcome this loss?
The insanity makes my head shake and cross
Help me, I plead in this world of debt
To overcome consciousness
Lay me in my tomb to rest
And hope that the world repairs at my request
Delay not I will find you
Overcome this shyness and I reward you
Help those in need, not those who want
It's incredible that you stare
Yet money is burning everywhere
You mine as well burn the Bible
Then don't say one syllable

Worthless

I didn't see it coming
When you took my hand and spoke to me
It was the end of life as I knew it
All comfort was gone from the world
Even those that I loved couldn't repair the pain
I am stuck, lifeless, nothing
Shout my name for it is worthless
Say these words for it is true
The grieving point has not come
But the desire to kill myself has never went away
I belong nowhere, you see
I'm a hollow shell that cannot be free
I finally belonged somewhere, but it's gone
I will never get it back
What do I do now?
Wait?

Wrong

An artist paints
A priest is a saint
But all I do is have complaints
What is wrong with me besides my bipolar?
Do I have schizophrenia or borderline disorder?
The choices are never-ending for me
Why hasn't God set me free?
To live like this is so confusing
I could just be a child fussing
And end up in a psych ward cussing
I pray to have God stand by my side in the fight and battle
But the ringing in my ear is a sound of a rattle
But I'm caged and slaughtered like cattle
What else could go wrong?

Feelings

Close my eyes and feel
My life is real
With every step I take
I will always make
A smile on my face
And descend into oblivion
Where hopes and dreams take action
I will heal my wounds
And escape every doom
That possesses a forthcoming to me
I feel powerless
Hopeless
Sightless
What deal did I make?
To play this part in life
I feel something all the time
It makes me sad
I look out the window
Hoping for release
To bide my time
And be part of the diseased

Unrealistic

Being famous is unrealistic
Having a smile all the time is unrealistic
Reading a book one page at a time is unrealistic
Saving time is unrealistic
Love at first sight is unrealistic
Dads sticking around is unrealistic
Breathing underwater is unrealistic
But most of all, being you is unrealistic

Fantasizing

I think in my head
Of all the wishes before I go to bed
I create characters in my mind
Imaginary friends are what I find
They get me through life when I am alone
They help me figure stuff out
They even help me when my suicide thoughts come out
They're always there when I need them
It's like I'm their flower, and they hold me up with their stem
I will always have them with me
Otherwise I will not be complete

Stressed Out

I make myself frantic
I sometimes start to panic
I'm Alive
But I don't feel it inside
School doesn't help my problems either way
Even if I go to therapy school, it is just okay
I feel like the world is never-ending
That everything is dying
So ask me why I'm stressed out
If this poem doesn't help, then shout
I will hear your call
And write another poem for all

The Rose

The cool wind brushes my face
The ground so soft in my safe place
Many trees move and sway
The wind whistles and moves you away
The flowers are dripping wet
The birds go to their nest
The animals say their goodbyes
The rain is coming but it is shy
Dripping rain makes a puddle lake
Until the ocean grows, that is what it makes
Every rose pours crimson and sadness
Going here you'll never forget
The peaceful sadness you'll regret
But the rose stays red all day long
Their beauty makes a song
Now everything stops

Loss

You're raining sadness
Everything is dark and depressing
The light that once showed is now gone
Every loving memory will stay with you
But saying goodbye is the hardest thing to do
Your eyes are all red and alone
Being yourself is not good at all
Knowing you'll never come back hurts my heart
I feel agony eating in my stomach
Every tear I pour is in agony of you
Saying hello to you felt like yesterday
But what about tomorrow
Nothing's the same anymore
Seeing your face, I'll never forget
The adventures you took, I was so impressed
Now you're in a happy place
But what about me
Can't survive without you
The sky outside is crying in memory of you
But you're gone

Shadow

Why couldn't he be around?
I never made a sound
Was he disappointed in me?
Why couldn't he help me?
He shouldn't be so selfish
All I wanted was a dad who cared
I didn't do anything; he is so unfair
Even though I should get over him
It feels if I love him, it should be a sin
Being daddy's little girl is all I ever wanted
But I guess he showed he didn't want it
A piece of my heart will never fill
Unless he comes back as a caring dad but still, until

Life

Life is where a human is born
That being will never be perfect or sure
No one knows what that child will grow up to be
It'll be normal or have a disease that no one will see
Its struggles may make history in the world
Or it can tear it apart and cause destruction to the world
Life is only a question
Maybe one person can find the connection
And solve the world problems
Could it be you?

Outside

Flowers slowly rain down
Every pettle swirls around
Rainbows slowly cross the sky
With fields of grass that go up so high
The deer prance through the woods
With the sound of trees swaying as they should
Nothing disturbs the peaceful field
With streams of flowers
Your dreams are real

Ignored

Sometimes I may be around a crowd I try to speak
My words are slurred with other people's speech
I feel alone and empty inside
Maybe I should hide
My feelings are crushed in my heart
I just want to fall apart
Being invisible shakes my world
For I am a sensitive girl
Maybe I should remain hidden
And say good ridden

Hopelessness

Never feeling happy again
My emotions mix and blend
No one's help, I am all alone
I might as well be stone
Treatments help for a while
But I want to run a mile
Being at the psych ward sucked
There is no such thing as luck
Nothing is going to get better, ever
I'll be like this forever
No escape, no way out
Still trying to figure it out
Other than that, there is nothing else

Alone

No one knows how I feel inside
I just want to hide
My past tears me in two
I have so many problems, what do I do
Talking about it never helps
Feels like I have been beaten by a belt
I feel hallow inside with no way out
I'm trapped in a forgotten cage, I can't even shout
Thoughts eat at my brain
Where there is nothing left but bloodstains
I'm all alone in the world
I'm a dark plague kind of girl

My Sister

My sister is your average sibling
Always pushing buttons and favoring
She knows what to say to make me mad
But other times she's sweet and makes me glad
Everything she does drives me insane
But hanging around her, I am never so sane
We have fights like every other sister
I'm glad I have her and not another
We can't be closer or farther apart
I enjoy every time with her and never want to depart
If she weren't my sister, I would never know life
I would never be whole or set for life
Through good times and bad, she is always there
Thank you

Heal

I will never heal, you will see
For my thoughts are so deep
Recovering from my memory is painful
It will take me years to become successful
I want a mind like everyone else
Other than that, I'm by myself
Going to therapy is a step to recovery
But sometimes I wonder if my pain is a new discovery
Reading books on bipolar will only teach me for a while
But going to the hospital is not my style
What do people think of me?
Am I crazy?
These questions need to be answered
Otherwise I will not heal
My pain is real
I'm stuck inside this body
And I will come out for nobody
That is why I will not heal

Depression

Cloudy days pass by me
Teardrops running down my face freely
Sitting in a dark corner is what I like to do
Being away from the world and all in it
Nobody understands my plea for help
Rainbows and unicorns are drowned by blood
A nagging in my stomach won't escape
I keep telling people how I feel
They can't possibly understand
The feeling of dying
The feeling of hopelessness
My whole world revolves around depression
I want to escape
But it is taking years to accomplish this task
I'm trying to help myself as best I can
Others deny I am doing anything at all
Then what is the point after all?

Hallucinations

Sitting at the computer by myself
I see an object move
It's not the cat for she is sleeping
I get up and go toward the object
A human figure approaches
Then vanishes
Nothing looks real anymore
I see objects of all sizes in my house that were never there
I want my eyes to clear of this nightmare
That is when I go straight to bed
And hope the hallucinations will end

Thoughts

Every thought fights with another
Until every speculation joins together
Racing suppositions stay in my head
None go absent until I go to bed
All these appraisals eat at my brain
Until there is nothing left but bloodstains

Dirty Looks

No matter where I go or what I do, I have a dirty look
My eyes jab you like a hook
All my feelings express through my face
For years, I've been trying to fix my surface
People see me as fierce and scary
I try to look at them nicely just barely
I tell myself I am happy
But really, I am unhappy
My face is a mirror to my world

Torture

Inside I say things to myself that do not help
I make myself hurt so bad like greeting a belt
Maybe I am the one causing destruction to myself
Just to make myself angry, I say ridiculous things
Afterward I feel like I have beestings
I do this every time I get my OCD
All the things I say I want to reorder
Still, I can't help myself and what I do
I'm a loner, that is true
Possibly I'll be like this forever

Anger

A fiery swell rises in my chest
I try to act nicely at my best
But the snap of rage in my face
Makes others feel unsafe
A tiny tap on my shoulder and I burst
And you will see me at my worst
Controlling it is out of the question
I'm possessed by my turbulence action
That overpowers every thought
Then I break all that I bought
How can I control this animosity?
If I can't be the boss of me
Calming down takes an hour
Then if I get mad again, I devour
It's hard to be around me
Cause at that point you'll want to flee
Happiness can never exist
If anger persists

Struggle

My heart and soul shred to a thousand pieces
Every bone deteriorates and collapses
The blood that once ran through my veins have drained
On the outside are smears and stains
The brain that was once there is now gone
The inside of me is all scattered along
My eyes roll back into my empty head
Now my skin starts to shed
Now I am dead

Bipolar

Being a teen with Bipolar completely bites
My mood swings go up and down like a kite
Anxiety and depression are always there
They stand out and are very clear
Students don't treat me nicely
Teachers help me most likely
There is no cure, so what can I do
I guess I have to live my life through
Every tiny thing annoys me
Other days I feel like dying
I'm all alone and by myself
In a huge hole with no way out
Tears cannot express what I feel
Nor can words
I'm stuck

Teenagers

Teenage years are dark and sad
No teen could possibly be glad
Adolescence and puberty are produced
Then anger and mood swings are introduced
Life was difficult in fourth grade
But these terms came around and stayed
My mood swings doubled and same with my anger
Being around me now is a danger
No one can treat it
So I just have to deal with it
Like everything else

Suicide

Life is so short when you make your time come
Life runs out before you become
A person should feel happy and glad
Not depressed and sad
So life comes to an end
With a slice to the head
Everything ends now
But why can't I do it now
Nothing's stopping me
Thoughts of killing myself are never-ending
Just one moment
That's all it takes
To end my life
No mistakes

Uncontrollable

Thoughts are racing in my brain
At that point I have no name
Shaking nonstop is what is happening
My brain stops, no more reacting
Crying so sweetly like death to a rose
Others have to make decisions for me, I suppose
Everything is spinning, why won't it stop
Stuck inside my head
I'm deprived so I go to bed
I need extreme help
Before I completely develop
Darkness falls everywhere
And everyone just stares
I'm at that point where there is no crying
People ask if I am okay, I say yes but I am denying
Being alone is comforting
But I am stuck to my thoughts always moving
There is no cure
I'm sure
The only way to go
Is death, I suppose

Expecting

People see me as sweet and nice
All my movements move around like ice
If I screw up one thing
People look at me differently
It is hard not to show anger and frustration
Some just want to see my reaction
But inside there is trouble and exhaust
I'm growing weeds and moss
All my bones are withering slowly
Inside my heart is very lonely
If people saw the real me, depression, upset, unhappy
They'd show different signs of respect
So then I act

Deserted

You've left me all alone in a bliss
Like the devil kissing my lips
It seems I have gone astray
All alone until the month of May
I see clearly as a rainbow
I'll come out so I can show
The world is at my fingertips
The way you left me is like a painful whip
I will be alone forever
Hoping one day we'll be together

Neglected

I don't take what is left of me
It seems so clear that you are here
Please you can save me if you tried
It feels like I have died
So why are you by me?
Look through the dirty mirror
And see your own horror

Writing

Every day I write in my journal
I sit around then pop ideas like kernel
I write everything down, you see
It makes me wonder and sets me free
Everyone should do it
Everyone has problems, just admit it
Journals solve everything out
Keeps your mind full and about
Getting everything down
It is great to have it around

Absent

I never show up at school
People look at me as if I was a fool
I usually miss days here or there
Then it comes to a point where I miss days everywhere
It's my anxiety, you see
Let me come back to school, help me please
I will go if I look forward to something
I won't go for no one or nothing

Impulse

Acting out
Shouting out
Saying things that are untrue
Saying things too soon
Speaking before thinking
Not even noticing
Until it is too late
You regret and hesitate
Knowing now the words have spilled
You might as well have your words be killed

Gray

The trees have lost all color
I just sit there and wonder
All the oceans and lakes are dull and plain
Have I gone insane?
My eyes wonder over the drab sky
I don't feel like myself, maybe I am high
Probably from all the medication I take
Maybe I took more by mistake
Inside my head is sawdust
Everything is taken out of me, even my lust

Disorder

I have many turmoils
They slip around like oils
My mayhems are complicated
For they all become affected
Every entanglement comes and goes
All of them fit me like shoes though
My disorganization is quite real
Yet again this is why I cannot heal
Every lawlessness has a reason
But right now is not the right season
Every dither is my own
Which I have shown
And will show probably the rest of my life
That is right

Melting

Sometimes my pain in my stomach just tares
Until I feel all bare
Then when I am upset, my insides light
I feel everything melting for it just might
Everything inside crashes down
My heart pounds
Fire rises in my chest
It closes in like a vest
Only suffocation remains
All I feel is pain
Until that cycle starts over once more
My anger scores
Everything's ablaze
Ashes slowly fall
That is it

Zero

Calling
Coming
Saving
Maybe
Lights dim at her sight
Zero seems inappropriate to say
But you may find her a bit fright
It will be a new day
Calling her for you just might
She'll sit down and lay
But Zero is her name
That nobody will say

Happiness

Happiness doesn't come by often
Like a person waiting for their train
But when it comes, I'll enjoy it
For it should be gone in a moment

Drama Queen

Semi-self-confident and overly dramatic describes me
One little incident and I enlarge the story
People see me as fun and laughter
But I see myself as boring and growing fatter
I drag on complaints to prolong my speech
But then I have to worry about my goals to reach
I sometimes tell my friends stories that aren't true
That helps the attention, that is what I do
People always find me strange
But I won't ever change
Being a drama queen is who I am
To over exaggerate and to always have fun

Full

Eating away my trouble
Will cause my weight to double
Comfort food isn't the answer
But afterward I feel better
Why can't I discontinue?
My eating is an issue
Soon, I'll be eating a little something
Then I'll be eating nothing

Divorce

A normal person would grieve in the loss of their parents' marriage
But I did not
What if the annulment meant nothing in my eyes?
I'm glad Daddy's gone
His presence weakened me
The total control on my family and me would be over
Even if that meant losing my dad

Whipped

Just that day you whipped me
I was a little girl and you whipped me
I was having fun, and a slash came across my back
You show no mercy but skill
I wish that you were dead
Embarrassed by the public
How could you do this, Daddy?
How can you live with yourself?
I didn't make a peep or a sound
When you flashed that belt around
I'm humiliated and ashamed
Go to hell

Dissection

Doctors have poked and prodded through my brain
They pore medication into my name
Doctors all around me
No escape, you see
I'm trapped within locked doors
Where they see all of the insides
Wondering how I am feeling
What is happening?
Too much pressure to deal with
They pick at my heart that beats slowly
I tell them everything
Just what they want, so they can do the experiment
Close me up please
I want out
But that is being Bipolar

Raped My Mind

Hearing every thought I think
Saying things to people before I speak
Searching for answers you cannot seek
My mind is naked, don't come near
Your whispers and chatting make me feel bare
Looking at me and laughing toward me
Makes me wonder if they can read me
Looking around with tears in my eyes
Everyone's laughing and know my secrets, I sigh
Please, God, help me and make me vanish
And let you vanquish this rape upon me
I just can't get them out of my head
They know everything now
I take a bow
Then stab myself good
Right through the heart

Firefly

Why can't I cry?
Maybe I am too shy
But even when I try
Something makes me want to fly
Fly away like a firefly
And wave everyone goodbye
But I still want to die
And hopefully meet a nice guy
Before I die
To help me change my mind
But maybe a firefly
Will someday
Help me to survive

Concentration

It's hard to focus and see
If there is a distraction all around me
Trying to remember is impossible
But just sitting is possible
I can't concentrate on anything
Noise can be heard everywhere

Family

Family should be kind and supporting
Not distant and reproaching
My family acts like a clique
I feel like I'm in school, they make me sick
They ignore and leave me unloved
I stay away and ask for help up above
My family never calls in time of need
I'm out of their portrait, yes indeed
Maybe this poem will help them see
Otherwise they'll let me be

# Manic

I'm on top of the world, nothing can stop me now
I don't need sleep anymore
I can do anything, I am sure
My head is above the clouds
And I am not coming down
Now I can put more words in a sentence
I move much faster in a shorter distance
Everyone's worries I completely forget
But now I am the main target
People look at me funny
But I'm all bright and sunny
I love me and who I am
Life is so wonderful, I can see stars now

Self-Esteem

Everyone says I have no self-esteem
I'm not bright and I don't gleam
All I do is follow others' feet
And say things while always missing a beat
Never raising my hand in class
If I do, I crash
I'm not arrogant or selfish
I'm quiet and helpless
I wish things could change
But I remain strange
I'm in this body so what can I do
I guess it is all up to you

Image

I look in the mirror and see fat and ugliness
Why can't I be sure of myself?
I feel insecure all the time
Except at bedtime
I'm too fat and have so many pimples
A diet and creams just seem so simple
But no matter how hard I try
I just feel disfigured inside
I want to hide behind a trash can
'Cause that is all I will ever feel for myself
Others deny my looks
But I despise how I look
Hopefully one day, I'll feel better
Otherwise life wouldn't matter

Crashes

The feeling of racing thoughts occurs
Others observe
You can't stop moving
Or sitting
Then you laugh over and over again
I feel like it is just pretend
Then there is the breakdown
Tears are then falling to the ground
Shaking uncontrollably
Who can help me now?
How much more can I allow?
Then I crash
Just staring at the trash

Alone

No one's ever around me
And when they are, they annoy me
Nothing can fill the empty loneliness
I would say how I feel, but it is no one's business
Thoughts racing inside as I am sitting alone
I'll probably be this way until I am nothing but bone

Scream

Pissed at the world and all in it
I beckon the day when you hit and spit at me
I rip my hair out wondering if you notice
That my world is crashing all around
Tearing up furniture and the house
It is like the exorcism has bellowed out
Hoping I will settle down
That the beast within will grow less hungry
Knowing there is no stopping me and what I've done
So I sit and scream

# *Dying Inside*

I sense there's something deep within
To hide what this monster made
All hope to die and be a lullaby
Have no cost and love to spare
Just waiting for the day
When justice prevails
But as the storm settles down
It is more than just a day
Finally, I stop breathing
No one finds the smears and stains
Blood lingers on my hair
Until nothing is left to say

Invincible

Run me over with a truck
I will sit in the street like a duck
Once I am run over, I will live
Nothing can harm me, nothing will
If I trip and fall, I will not bleed
For I am just a tiny seed
That will live forever
I will be bright and known until they discover
That I am Bipolar

Eyes

Beautiful, oh, they may seem
Brightly hazel ever seen
They look around with curiosity and wonder
Then sear right through you with deep somber
Help these eyes say
They don't seem to be okay
She cries crimson and blood
For she thought she was beautiful and loved
Her eyes can be seen a thousand miles away
But she will still cry today

Applaud the Chains

I know the truth behind
Your secret alibi
Things are not what they appear
I test you not to disappear
Raging inside my aching heart
Ready for the game to start
Pull out your weapons and show me your mask
If you want to die, just ask
Steady and slowly you light the candle
You put your hand on the crooked mantle
The chains are coming, just you wait
This is your final state
You're evil and insane
So Applaud the Chains

I Am Me

No matter what people say
No matter how hard I work
I will always be me
Never following drugs
Only asking for hugs
I'm my own person, you see
That one day I'll be bright as the sea
I don't go with others' fashion
I'm sweet, that is no question
I will always be me
Others may talk and say I'm unsocial
But my fantasy takes me away
At night, I dream of my bright future
And help others that need my attention
I will always be me
And no matter how hard people want me to change
They'll have to accept me
The way I am

Unique

What is so unique about me?
My imagination runs freely
I'm not a girl who runs from trouble
Unless my problems double
Time doesn't show who I am
I just come out like a clam
Until I realized I am not the only one
I have not won until I am done

Invisible

Slam right through me
See right through me
I am bacteria in the air
I am a child, so unfair
There is sand in the water
I am unpredictable
Eyes glaze in a steady haze
I am lost within the maze
So many eyes moving about
They can't find me even if I shout
Invisible, invisible, invisible,
They say
Some will have noticed
Others will have wondered
But I will be astray
They say

Love

Wonders upon wonders
Dreams upon dreams
The world goes round
My heart stays bound
But crystals fly through the air
Not stopping even if they dare
Your dreams are real
That will bind a seal
With your heart

Triggers

In the rooms are seals
Surrounded by people who are real
What they discuss may cause a flinch
Your emotions run high and you might move an inch
Crying now, your tears are special
Running out the door, your footsteps echo
And that's it, that's all
Now it's time to go to the ball

Movie Star Crush

Boys make my stomach flip
And I'll never forget
The way their eyes look into mine
Even though it is a poster, he's fine
I like the curly locks in his hair
I would love to feel it or just stare
The six-pack on his stomach makes me melt
The papery touch is all I felt
That million-dollar smile
Is always in style
I will never forget my first love
Out of all the pictures he's above
I'll save his face forever
And dream we'll be together

Psychiatric Ward

A place where mentally ill come
It is a place to help you become
Always being watched
Always getting caught
No sharp objects allowed
Or you'll have to do a body check right now
Always in groups
Marching in like troops
All here for a purpose
Drug addicts, alcoholics, suicide, and depression
Getting out is everyone's obsession
Locked doors
How much more?
Then code yellow
What a lucky fellow
To shout and bellow
Being strapped to a bed
Why can't you just talk about it instead?
Welcome to the Psych Ward

Untitled

Puking up my guts
Then covering up my cuts
I use anything I can to feel pain
But again, it is all the same
Wishing I were dead
But living instead
Hating myself but loving others
I try to hide my scars so I duck and cover
Going to the hospital helps, sometimes
It helps me get away for a moment in time
When my mind goes and fights
I take on a battlefield with flashing lights
But those are just sirens
To take me away
In the psych ward
Where I can stay
And hopefully get better
I pray

Human

I'm only human, so they say
Blood rushes through my veins
So I guess that makes me part of the living
Even though I am bipolar and giving

Black Heart

I'm not good all the time
The colors of my heart change like slime
I'm usually obedient and nice
But watch what you say to me, think twice
That I can be cruel and mishearted
But I'm ready to get started
I have a black heart, you see
So with this heart, I am not free

Nothing

Nothing to say, nothing to write
I'm all out of ideas, now you have doubts
Tearful moments prosper
Sighs seem improper
This is a poem, right?
Then why does it seem so affright
All the ingredients in this poem make the ideal nothing
I might as well be subtracting
Into nothingness of all the land
Then fill your heart for it is bland
Miles away seem so little and bleak
You might as well be subliminal and weak
Don't surprise yourself for a cause
Because all is perfect from a pause

Uncle Bob

So strong and funny
I remember that day
When you dropped me on my head
You'd scream Aunt Carol's name
And she immediately came
You made me laugh all the time
Your funny jokes rang like a chime
But now you're gone into heaven
Say hello to God because you'll be with him
I miss you like you don't know
I'd really wish you'd show
You'll miss out on walking me down the aisle
You'll miss my children grow up
Why'd you have to leave me?
Why'd you have to go?
But now I have to remember
You're not suffering anymore
I'm happy for you
You don't even know
But now it is time to say goodbye
I don't dare speak these words out loud
I don't want to make a sound
But I'm ready to say this once and for all
Goodbye, I will be strong

About the Author

Jessica Marion King lives in Illinois with her mother and older sister. She is very family oriented and aspires to be a great author one day with the help of her imagination and experiences in life. In her free time, besides writing, she loves to read, play with her dog, take long walks, and just spend time with her loved ones.